100% Blonde Jokes:

The Best Dumb, Funny, Clean, Short and Long Blonde Jokes Book

R. Cristi

Author Online!

For updates and more jokes
visit R. Cristi page at

www.bestjokebooks.com

100% Blonde Jokes:
The Best, Most Funny, Dumb Blonde Jokes Ever
by **R. Cristi**

ISBN 978-0-9866004-1-8

Printed in the United States of America

Also by R. Cristi

100% SMS Jokes
(Forthcoming)

100% Short Jokes
(Forthcoming)

100% Mexican Jokes
(Forthcoming)

Give Her Another Chance

One day a big group of blondes met in New York to show the world that blondes aren't dumb.
They begged: "Ask any of us any question, and we will show you that we're not dumb."

The group caught the attention of a passer by, who volunteered to ask them some questions. He climbed up on a car and randomly picked a blonde out of the crowd.

She got up on the car too and the man asked: "What is the first month of the year?"
The blonde responded: "November?"

"Nope," said the man. At this point the crowd began to chant, "Give her another chance, give her another chance."

So the man asked: "What is the capital of the USA ?"
The blonde responded: "Paris?"
So the crowd began chanting again: "Give her another chance, give her another chance."

The man said: "Okay, but this is the last one. What is one plus one?"
The blonde replied: "Two?"

"Give her another chance, Give her another chance." screamed the crowd.

New Cell Phone

A blonde gets a new cell phone from her husband.

The next day she goes to Wal-Mart and her phone rings, so she answers it.

It was her husband. He says, "How's the new cell phone?"

She replied, "Great...but how did you know I was at Wal-Mart?"

Mind Telling Me the Time?

Blonde: "Excuse me, what time is it right now?"

Woman: "It's 11:25PM."

Blonde: (confused look on face) "You know, it's the weirdest thing, I've asked that question thirty times today, and every time someone gives me a different answer."

Passed Away

Sally goes to work one morning crying her eyes out. Her boss, concerned his employee, walks over to her and asks sympathetically, "What's the matter?" The blonde replies, "Early this morning I got a phone call that my mother had passed away."

The boss, feeling very sorry at this point suggests to the young girl, "Why don't you go home for the day... we aren't terribly busy. Just take the day off and go relax."

Sally very calmly states, "No I'd be better off here. I need to keep my mind busy and I have the best chance of doing that here."

The boss agrees and allows her to work as usual. "If you need anything just let me know" says the boss.

A few hours pass and the boss decides to check on Sally. He looks out his office and sees her crying hysterically.

He rushes over an asks, "What's the matter now? Are you going to be OK?"

Sally breaks down in tears. "I just received a horrible call from my sister. She said that her mom died too!!"

Blonde Interview

A blonde airhead goes for a job interview in an office. The interviewer starts with the basics.

"So, Miss, can you tell us your age, please?"

The blonde counts carefully on her fingers for half a minute before replying "Ehhhh... 22!"

The interviewer tries another straightforward one to break the ice. "And can you tell us your height, please?"

The young lady stands up and produces a measuring tape from her handbag. She then traps one end under her foot and extends the tape to the top of her head. She checks the measurement and announces "Five foot two!"

This isn't looking good so the interviewer goes for the real basics; something the interviewee won't have to count, measure, or look up. "Just to confirm for our records, your name please?"

The airhead bobs her head from side to side for about ten seconds, mouthing something silently to herself, before replying "MANDY!"

The interviewer is completely baffled at this stage, so he asks "What in the world were you doing when I asked you your name?"

"Ohhhh, that!" replies the airhead, "I was just running through that song - 'Happy birthday to you, happy birthday to you, happy birthday dear...'"

Speeding Ticket

A blonde was speeding on the highway when a police car pulled her over.

The policeman walks up to the blonde and says "Excuse m'am, could I please see your driving license and registration."

The blonde looks at the policeman angrily and says "I wish you guys would get your act together. Just yesterday you take away my license and then today you expect me to show it to you!"

A Smart Blonde Joke

A blonde walks into a bank in New York City and asks for the loan officer. She says she's going to Europe on business for two weeks and needs to borrow $5,000.

The bank officer says the bank will need some kind of security for the loan, so the blonde hands over the keys to a new Mercedes Benz SL 500.

The car is parked on the street in front of the bank, she has the title and everything checks out. The bank agrees to accept the car collateral for the loan.

The bank's president and its officers all enjoy a good laugh at the blond for using a $110,000 Benz as collateral against a $5,000 loan.

An employee of the bank then proceeds to drive the Benz into the bank's underground garage and parks it there. Two weeks later, the blonde returns, repays the $5,000 and the interest, which comes to $15.41.

The loan officer says, "Miss, we are very happy to have had your business, and this transaction has worked out very nicely, but we are a little puzzled. While you were away, we checked you out and found that you are a multimillionaire.

What puzzles us is, why would you bother to borrow $5,000?"

The blonde replies, "Where else in New York City can I park my car for two weeks for only $15.41 and expect it to be there when I return?"

Finally... a smart blonde joke.

At the Bus Stop

Two blonds are waiting at a bus stop.

When a bus pulls up and opens the door, one of the blonds leans inside and asks the bus driver: "Will this bus take me to 5th Avenue?"

The bus driver shakes his head and says, "No, I'm sorry."

Hearing this, the other blond leans inside, smiles, and twitters:

"Will it take ME?"

Blonde Shoots Herself

A blonde hurries into the emergency room late one night with the tip of her index finger shot off.

"How did this happen?" the emergency room doctor asked her.

Well, I was trying to commit suicide, the blonde replied.

"What?" sputtered the doctor. "You tried to commit suicide by shooting your finger off?"

"No, Silly!" the blonde said. "First I put the gun to my chest, and I thought: I just paid $6,000.00 for these breast implants, I'm not shooting myself in the chest."

"And then?" asked the doctor.

"Then I put the gun in my mouth, and I thought: I just paid $3000.00 to get my teeth straightened, I'm not shooting myself in the mouth."

"And then?"

"Then I put the gun to my ear, and I thought: This is going to make a loud noise. So I put my finger in the other ear before I pulled the trigger."

Blonde Guy

A blonde guy gets home early from work and hears strange noises coming from the bedroom. He rushes upstairs to find his wife naked on the bed, sweating and panting. "What's up?" he says. "I'm having a heart attack," cries the woman.

He rushes downstairs to grab the phone, but just as he's dialing, his 4-year-old son comes up and says, "Daddy! Daddy! Uncle Ted's hiding in your closet and he's got no clothes on!"

The guy slams the phone down and storms upstairs into the bedroom, past his screaming wife, and rips open the wardrobe door.

Sure enough, there is his brother, totally naked, cowering on the closet floor.

You rotten bastard, "says the husband, "my wife's having a heart attack and you're running around naked scaring the kids!

Non-Stop Flight

On a plane flight from Seattle to Chicago, a blonde was sitting in economy class. About half way through the flight, she got up and moved to an empty seat in first class. A flight attendant who observed this, went over to her and politely explained that she had to move back to economy class because that was what her ticket was for. The blonde replied, "I'm blonde, I'm beautiful, I'm going to Chicago and I'm staying right here."

After several attempts to explain to the blonde why she had to return to economy class, the flight attendant gave up. She went to the cockpit and explained the situation to the pilot and co-pilot. The co-pilot said, "Let me try." He went up to the blonde and politely tried to explain to her why she needed to return to her seat in economy class.

But the blonde only replied, "I'm blonde, I'm beautiful, I'm going to Chicago and I'm staying right here." Frustrated, the co-pilot returned to the cockpit. He suggested that perhaps they should have the airline call the police and have her arrested when they land.

"Wait a minute," said the pilot. "Did you say she's blonde? I can handle this. My wife is a blonde. I speak Blonde." So he went up to the woman sitting in first class and whispered something in her ear.

"I'm sorry," said the blonde, and she promptly got up and returned to her seat in economy class.

"What did you say to her?" ask the astonished flight attendant and co-pilot.

To which the pilot replied, "I just told her that first class isn't going to Chicago."

How Do I Get Across That River?

A dumb blonde is walking along, lost, and encounters a deep and wide river. She looks up and down the river for a way across but is unsuccessful in finding one. Yet, when looking to the other side again, she happened to see another blonde on the opposite river bank. She tried calling to her.

"How can I get to the other side of the river?" she shouts loudly.

The other blonde replied "What for? You are already on the other side of the river!"

The Mini Skirt

In a crowded city at a busy bus stop, a beautiful young woman who was waiting for a bus was wearing a tight mini skirt.

As the bus stopped and it was her turn to get on, she became aware that her skirt was too tight to allow her leg to come up to the height of the first step of the bus.

Slightly embarrassed and with a quick smile to the bus driver, she reached behind her to unzip her skirt a little, thinking that this would give her enough slack to raise her leg.

Again, she tried to make the step only to discover she still couldn't.

So, a little more embarrassed, she once again reached behind her to unzip her skirt a little more, and for the second time attempted the step, and, once again, much to her dismay, she could not raise her leg.

With a little smile to the driver, she again reached behind a third time to unzip a little more and again was unable to make the step.

About this time, a large Texan who was standing behind her picked her up easily by the waist and placed her gently on the step of the bus.

She went ballistic and turned to the would be Samaritan and yelled, "How dare you touch my body! I don't even know who you are!"

The Texan smiled and drawled, "Well, ma'am, normally I would agree with you, but after you unzipped my fly three times, I kinda figured we was friends!"

Yes, No, Yes, No, Yes...

This guy was driving in a car with a blonde. He told her to stick her head out the window and see if the blinker worked.

She stuck her head out and said, 'Yes, No, Yes, No, Yes...'

Two Blondes In Heaven

One blond says to another, "how did you die"?

"I froze to death," says the second.

"That's awful" says the first blonde. "How does it feel to freeze to death?"

"It's very uncomfortable at first," says the second blonde. "You get the shakes, and you get pains in all your fingers and toes. But eventually, it's a very calm way to go. You get numb and you kind of drift off, as if you're sleeping."

"How about you, how did you die?" asked the second blonde.

"I had a heart attack," says the first blonde. "You see I knew my husband was cheating on me, so one day I showed up at home unexpectedly. I ran up to the bedroom, and found him alone watching TV. I ran to the basement, but no one was hiding there either. I ran to the second floor, but no one was hiding there either. I ran as fast as I could to the attic, and just as I got there, I had a massive heart attack and died.

The second blonde shakes her head. "What a pity ... if you had only looked in the freezer, we'd both still be alive."

Another Blonde Police Applicant

A blonde walks into the police department looking for a job. The captain says they can't just turn her away, and orders to desk officer to ask her a few questions as if doing an interview.

Not having any idea what to ask her to disqualify her application, the officer asks, "What's 2+2?"

"Ummm... 4!" the blonde says.

Dang, the officer thinks, so tries a harder one: "What's the square root of 100?"

"Ummm... 10!" the blonde says.

"Good!" the officer says, deciding to switch from math to history. "OK, who killed Abraham Lincoln?"

"Ummm... I don't know," she admits.

"Well, you can go home and think about it," he says, "and come back later and tell me what you've figured out." He figures that's the last he'll see of her.

The blonde goes home and calls up one of her friends, who asks her if she got the job.

"Not only did I get the job," the blonde says, "but I've already been assigned to a murder case!"

Blonde at Football Game

A guy decides to bring his new blonde girlfriend to a football game. After the game is over, he asks her if she liked the game.

She replies: "Oh it was great, I loved watching those men in tight clothes, but there is one thing I don't understand."

"What did you not understand ?"

And the blonde says: "Well, at the beginning of the game, both teams flipped a quarter to see who would kick off first. Then the rest of the game everybody was yelling get the quarter back, get the quarter back, get the quarter back. So I thought to myself, gosh it's just a quarter!"

Hot and Cold

A blonde was shopping when she found a really striking stainless steel thermos. Fascinated, she picked it up examined it, and finally asked the clerk what it was.

"It's a thermos." he said. "It keeps some things hot, and other things cold."

That was all she needed to hear, and she bought the thermos.

The next day, her boss saw the thermos on her desk, as it really was rather striking.

"What's that?" her boss asked.

"It's a thermos." she said. "It keeps some things hot, and other things cold."

"What have you got in it?" her boss queried after a moment.

She happily answered, "I have hot coffee in it for a little later this morning, and really cold iced tea for this afternoon."

Magic Mirror

There was this bar and in the bar there was a magic mirror.

If you told a lie it would suck you in.

One day a brunette walked into this bar. She walked up to the mirror and said 'I think I'm the most beautiful woman in the world' and it sucked her in.

The next day a redhead walked into the bar. She walked up to the mirror and said 'I think I'm the most beautiful woman in the world' and it sucked her in.

Then the next day a blond walked into the bar. She walked up to the mirror and said 'I think...' and it sucked her in.

Oklahoma Blondes

Two blondes living in Oklahoma were sitting on a bench talking ... and one blonde says to the other, "Which do you think is farther away ... Florida or the moon?"

The other blonde turns and says "Hellooooooooooo, can you see Florida ...?"

Donations

A blonde, brunette, and redhead went to a church to donate money. The brunette draws a circle around her and throws up all her money.

She says that whatever lands inside the circle is for God, and whatever lands outside of the circle she keeps.

The redhead then draws a line, stands on it, and throws up all of her money. She said that whatever lands on the right side of the line is for God, and whatever lands on the left side she keeps.

The blonde throws up her money, and yells, "God, whatever you catch is yours, and whatever you don't I get to keep."

Do You See the Dead Bird?

A brunette and a blonde are walking along in a park one morning.

Suddenly, the brunette notices a dead bird. "Awww, look at the dead birdie," she says sadly.

The blonde stops, looks up into the sky, and says, "Where? Where?"

The Lumberyard

Two blondes drive into a lumberyard. The passenger gets out of the truck, walks up to a worker, and says she needs a bunch of four-by-twos.

"You mean two-by-fours?" the worker asks.

"Hm, I'm not sure," the blonde says. "I'll go check."

She walks back to the truck, and the two blondes consult a book.

"Yeah," she says after getting the answer. "I meant two-by-fours."

"All right," says the worker. "How long do you need them?"

This time, the sweet young thing didn't even need to consult the book.

"A really long time," she says. "We're gonna build a house."

Watch Dogs

A blonde was walking her dogs when a man walking in the opposite direction says "oh my, you have such beautiful dogs.. what are their names?"

The blonde replies "Well, the taller one is Timex and the shorter one is Rolex."

The man responds "Huh.. that's interesting.. why did you name them such names?"

The blonde sighs and shakes her head "Everyone keeps asking me the same thing... duhh, what else can you name your watch dogs?"

One Minute

A British Airways employee took a call from a blonde asking the question, "How long is the Concorde flight from London to New York?"

"Um, just a minute, if you please," he murmured.

Then, as he turned to check the exact flight time, he heard an equally polite, "Thank you," as the phone went dead.

Shortage of Parachutes

A blonde, a brunette, a movie star, the pope, and a pilot were on a plane.

The plane was going down fast, and there were only four parachutes for all five of them.

The pilot took one and jumped, then the movie star took one and jumped, and then the blonde took one and jumped.

The pope told the brunette to take the last one.

The brunette said, "There are still 2 parachutes left! The blonde took my backpack!"

Library Fast Food

A blonde went in the library and walked up to the librarian behind the desk and said, "I would like a cheeseburger."

The librarian replied,"Shh! This is a library!"

The blonde blushed. "oh, sorry.." then she whispered, "I would like a cheeseburger."

Brain For Sale

A client of a hospital where they made brain transplantation asked about the prices.

The doctor said, "Well, this Ph.D. brain costs $10,000. This brain belonged to a NASA top scientist and costs $15,000. Here we have a blonde's brain as well. It costs $50,000."

The client asked, "What? How's that possible?"

The doctor replied, "You see, it's totally unused."

Blonde Father

A blonde guy and a brunette girl were happily married and about to have a baby. One day, the wife started having contractions, so the husband rushed her to the hospital. He held her hand as she went through a trying birth. In the end, there were two little baby boys.

The blonde guy turned to his wife and angrily said, "All right, who's the other father!?!"

Million Dollar Answer

A contestant on 'Who Wants to be a Millionaire?' had reached the final plateau. If she answered the next question correctly, she would win the million dollars. If she answered incorrectly, she would pocket only the $32,000 milestone money.

And as she suspected it would be, the million-dollar question was no pushover. It was, "Which of the following species of birds does not build its own nest, but instead lays its eggs in the nests of other birds? Is it:

A) the condor;
B) the buzzard;
C) the cuckoo;
D) the vulture?"

The woman was on the spot. She did not know the answer. And she was doubly on the spot because she had used up her 50/50 Lifeline and her Audience Poll Lifeline. All that remained was her Phone-a-Friend Lifeline, and the woman had hoped against hope that she would not have to use it. Mainly because the only friend that she knew would be home happened to be a blonde.

But the contestant had no alternative. She called her

friend and gave her the question and the four choices. The blonde responded unhesitatingly: "That's easy. The answer is 'C' -- the cuckoo."

The contestant had to make a decision and make it fast. She considered employing a reverse strategy and giving Regis any answer except the one that her friend had given her. And considering that her friend was a blonde, that would seem to be the logical thing to do.

On the other hand, the blonde had responded with such confidence, such certitude, that the contestant could not help but be persuaded.

Time was up. "I need an answer," said Regis.

Crossing her fingers, the contestant said, "C) the cuckoo."

"Is that your final answer?" asked Regis.

"Yes, that is my final answer," she said, breaking into a sweat.

After the usual foot-dragging delay Regis said, "I regret to inform you that that answer is ... absolutely correct. You are now a millionaire!"

Three days later, the contestant hosted a party for her family and friends, including the blonde who had helped her win the million dollars.

"Jenny, I just do not know how to thank you," said the contestant. "Because of your knowing the answer to that final question, I am now a millionaire. And do you want to know something? It was the assuredness with which you answered the question that convinced me to go with your choice."

"You're welcome!" the blonde said.

"By the way," the winner said, not being able to contain the question anymore. "How did you happen to know the right answer?"

"Oh, come on," said the blonde. "Everybody knows that cuckoos don't build nests. They live in clocks."

Playing Trivial Pursuit

A blonde was playing Trivial Pursuit one night. It was her turn. She rolled the dice and she landed on Science and Nature. Her question was, "If you are in a vacuum and someone calls your name, can you hear it?"

She thought for a time and then asked, "Is it on or off?"

Where is the Bathroom?

One day, a brunette walked into a gas station and asked the cashier, "Where is the bathroom?" The cashier replied, "It's all the way in the back, but there's no toilet paper so you have to use a dollar."
So, she goes to the bathroom and walks out of the gas station.

A redhead walks in. She asked the cashier where the bathroom was. He said the same thing. "it's all the way in the back but there's no toilet paper so you have to use a dollar." So, the redhead goes to the bathroom and walks out of the gas station.

A blonde walks in and asks where the bathroom is. The cashier replied,"It's all the way in the back but there's no toilet paper so you have to use a dollar."

The blonde goes to the bathroom and come out moaning. "Whats wrong?" The cashier said. "I didn't have a dollar so I used quarters."

Someone Should Give Him Head & Shoulders

A blonde and a brunette are both in an elevator.

On the third floor a man gets on who's perfect: Italian suit, handsome, great build with a nice butt, but unfortunately they both notice he has a bad case of dandruff.

The man gets off on the 5th floor.

Once the doors close, the brunette turns to the blonde and says, "Someone should give him Head & Shoulders."

To which the blonde replies, "How do you give Shoulders?"

The Blonde In The Library

A blonde walked up to the front desk of the library and said, "I borrowed a book last week, but it was the most boring I've ever read. There was no story whatsoever, and there were far too many characters!"

The librarian replied, "Oh, you must be the person who took our phone book."

The Circle

A blonde has just gotten a new sports car. She cuts out in front of a semi, and almost causes it to drive over a cliff. The driver furiously motions for her to pull over, and she does. The driver gets out and draws a circle and tells her to stand in it. Then he gets out his knife and cuts up her leather seats. He turns around and sees she's smiling. So he goes to his truck, takes out a baseball bat, and starts busting her windows and beating her car. He looks back to see that she's laughing. He's really mad now, so he takes his knife and slices her tires. He turns around and she's laughing so hard, she's about to fall down.

He demands, "What's so funny?"

She says, "Every time you weren't looking, I stepped out of the circle!"

Lesbian

A blonde guy was sitting in a bar when he spots a very pretty young woman. He advances towards her when the bartender says to him, "Don't waste your time on that one. She's a lesbian."

The blonde goes over to her anyway and says, "So which part of Lesbia are you from?"

Pregnancy Test

The blonde had been married about a year when one day she came running up to her husband jumping for joy.

Not knowing how to react, the husband started jumping up and down along with her. "Why are we so happy?" he asked.

She said, "Honey, I have some really great news for you!"

"Great" he said, "tell me what you're so happy about."

She stopped breathless from all the jumping up and down. "I'm pregnant!" she gasped.

The husband was ecstatic as they had been trying for a while. He grabbed her, kissed her, and started telling her how wonderful it was, and that he couldn't be happier.

Then she said "Oh, honey there's more."

"What do you mean more?", he asked.

"Well we are not having just one baby, we are going to have TWINS!"

Amazed at how she could know so soon after getting pregnant, he asked her how she knew.

"It was easy" she said, "I went to the pharmacy and bought the 2 pack home pregnancy test kit and both tests came out positive!"

The Wal-Mart Cat

A blonde was weed-eating her yard and accidentally cut off the tail of her cat, which was hiding in the grass.

She rushed her cat, along with the tail, over to Wal-Mart!

Why Wal-Mart, you ask?

Hellooooooooo!

Wal-Mart is the largest retailer in the world!

New Puppy

Two blondes went to the pound where each adopted a puppy. The joy of their new best friend was quickly overshadowed when they got home and the first blonde said, "I think we're in trouble, how are we going to tell them apart?"

This lead to several hours of concentration until finally, the second blonde said, "I've got an idea. We'll tie a red bow around my puppy and a blue bow around yours."

The next day the first blonde comes running up to the second when she got home, "Oh no, I can't tell whose puppy is whose. They've pulled the ribbons off while they were playing."

"OK, we need to find a better way to tell them apart," says the second blonde.   After several more hours of concentration, they came up with the bright idea of getting different colored collars.

Again, the next day, the first blonde comes running up to the second as soon as she gets home, "Oh no, I can't tell whose puppy is whose. They've pulled their collars off while they were playing."

"There's got to be some way to tell them apart," says the second blonde.

After several more hours of concentration, the first blonde finally comes up with another idea, "I know! Why don't you take the black one and I'll take the white one!"

Just Plain Dumb

A blonde and a redhead were sitting together having drinks, when the blonde noticed a man walking towards them with an arm full of long stem red roses. The blonde says to the redhead, "isn't that your husband coming carrying all those roses?"

The redhead says, yes it is.

The blonde responds by saying, "Oh you are so lucky".

The redhead says, "No I'm not. All that means is that I have to spend the whole week-end flat on my back, with my legs in the air and spread apart."

The blonde says, "Oh my, don't you have a vase to put them in"?

I Can't Breathe Without That

A blonde goes into the beauty and hair parlor with her walkman on her head.

"I need to take that walkman off your head," says the beauty specialist as she notices the blonde.

"You can't! I'll die!" retorts the blonde.

"I can't cut your hair with the walkman on your ears!" says the beauty specialist getting annoyed.

"I said you can't take it off, or I'll die!"

The beauty specialist, outraged and flustered, grabs the walkman and throws it off the head of the blonde. Within seconds, the blonde dies. When the specialist picks up the walkman to listen, she hears it repeating "breath in, breath out, breath in".

Blonde Painting the House

This blonde decides one day that she is sick and tired of all these blonde jokes and how all blondes are perceived as stupid, so she decides to show her husband that blondes really are smart. While her husband is off at work, she decides that she is going to paint a couple of rooms in the house.

The next day, right after her husband leaves for work, she gets down to the task at hand. Her husband arrives home at 5:30 and smells the distinctive smell of paint. He walks into the living room and finds his wife lying on the floor in a pool of sweat. He notices that she is wearing a ski jacket and a fur coat at the same time.

He goes over and asks her if she is OK. She replies yes. He asks what she is doing. She replies that she wanted to prove to him that not all blonde women are dumb and she wanted to do it by painting the house. He then asks her why she has a ski jacket over her fur coat. She replies that she was reading the directions on the paint can and they said....

FOR BEST RESULTS, PUT ON TWO COATS.

3 People in a Airplane

Once there were 3 people in an airplane, one took a bite out of an apple. She thought it was too sweet so she threw it out of the plane.

The second person took a bite out of a lemon and she thought it was too sour so, she threw it out of the plane.

Then the last person took a bite out of a grenade and he thought it was too crunchy so, he threw it out of the plane.

Then they landed and decided to go for a walk. They first passed a little girl who was crying and they asked, "little girl, little girl, why are you crying?" and the little girl said, "an apple came down and killed my new kitty".

Next they passed a little boy who was also crying. And they again asked, "little boy, little boy, why are you crying?" and the little boy said, "a lemon came down and killed my new puppy."

Then they passed a blonde sitting on the side walk laughing her butt off. They asked, "why are you laughing so hard?" and the blonde said, "I farted and the building behind me blew up!"

Blonde Year

January - Took new scarf back to store because it was too tight.

February - Fired from pharmacy job for failing to print labels... "duh"... bottles won't fit in typewriter!

March - Got excited! Finished jigsaw puzzle in 6 months... box said "2-4 years!"

April - Trapped on escalator for hours... power went out!

May - Tried to make Kool-Aid. 8 cups of water won't fit into those little packets!

June - Tried to go water skiing. Couldn't find a lake with a slope.

July - Lost breast stroke swimming competition. Learned later, other swimmers cheated, they used their arms!

August - Got locked out of car in rain storm. Car swamped, because top was down.

September - The capital of California is "C"... isn't it?

October - Hate M & M's! They are so hard to peel.

November - Baked turkey for 4 1/2 days. Instructions said 1 hour per pound and I weigh 108!

December - Couldn't call 911... "duh"... there's no "eleven" button on the phone!

What a year!

Civic Lesson

In a high school civics class, they were discussing the qualifications for becoming President of the United States. The requirements are pretty simple. The candidate must be a natural born citizen and at least 35 years old.

A blonde girl in the class piped up and began complaining about how unfair it was to require the candidate to be a natural born citizen. In her opinion, that made it impossible for many qualified people to run for the office. She went on and on, wrapping up her argument with "What makes a natural born citizen more qualified to be President than one born by C-Section?"

Game Of Intelligence

There was a blonde who found herself sitting next to a lawyer on an airplane. The lawyer just kept bugging the blonde wanting her to play a game of intelligence. Finally, the lawyer offered her 10 to 1 odds, and said every time the blonde could not answer one of his questions, she owed him $5, but every time he could not answer hers, he'd give her $50.00. The lawyer figured he could not lose, and the blonde reluctantly accepted.

The lawyer first asked, "What is the distance between the Earth and the nearest star?"

Without saying a word the blonde handed him $5. then the blonde asked, "What goes up a hill with 3 legs and comes back down the hill with 4 legs?"

Well, the lawyer looked puzzled. He took several hours, looking up everything he could on his laptop and even placing numerous air-to-ground phone calls trying to find the answer. Finally, angry and frustrated, he gave up and paid the blonde $50.00

The blonde put the $50 into her purse without comment, but the lawyer insisted, "What is the answer to your question?"

Without saying a word, the blonde handed him $5.

History Lesson

A noted psychiatrist was a guest at a blonde gathering, and his hostess naturally broached the subject in which the doctor was most at ease.

"Would you mind telling me, Doctor," she asked, "how you detect a mental deficiency in somebody who appears completely normal?"

"Nothing is easier," he replied. "You ask him a simple question which everyone should answer with no trouble. If he hesitates, that puts you on the track."

"What sort of question?"

"Well, you might ask him, 'Captain Cook made three trips around the world and died during one of them. Which one?'

The blonde thought a moment, then said with a nervous laugh, "You wouldn't happen to have another example would you? I must confess I don't know much about history."

You Gotta Jump

A brunette, a redhead and a blonde escape a burning building by climbing to the roof. Firemen are on the street below, holding a blanket for them to jump in. The firemen yell to the brunette, "Jump! Jump! It's your only chance to survive!" The brunette jumps and SWISH! The firemen yank the blanket away. The brunette slams into the sidewalk like a tomato.

"C'mon! Jump! You gotta jump!" say the firemen to the redhead.

"Oh no! You're gonna pull the blanket away!" says the redhead.

"No! It's brunettes we can't stand! We're OK with redheads!"

"OK," says the redhead, and she jumps. SWISH! The firemen yank the blanket away, and the lady is flattened on the pavement like a pancake.

Finally, the blonde steps to the edge of the roof. Again, the firemen yell, "Jump! You have to jump!"

"No way! You're just gonna pull the blanket away!" yelled the blonde.

"No! Really! You have to jump! We won't pull the blanket away!"

"Look," the blonde says. "Nothing you say is gonna convince me that you're not gonna pull the blanket away! So what I want you to do is put the blanket down, and back away from it..."

Indecent Exposure

A blonde is walking down the street with her blouse open and her right breast hanging out. A policeman approaches her and says, "Ma'am, are you aware that I could cite you for indecent exposure?"

She says, "Why, officer?"

"Because your breast is hanging out."

She looks down and says, "OH MY GOODNESS! I left the baby on the bus again!"

I Want Some Milk

Gloria the blonde once heard that milk baths would make you beautiful. She left a note for her milkman Alan to leave 15 gallons of milk.

When Alan read the note, he felt there must be a mistake. He thought she probably meant 1.5 gallons, so he knocked on the door to clarify the order.

Gloria came to the door, and Alan said, "I found your note to leave 15 gallons of milk. Did you mean 15 gallons or 1.5 gallons?"

Gloria said, "I want 15 gallons. I'm going to fill my bathtub up with milk and take a milk bath."

Alan asked, "Oh, alright, would you like it pasteurized?"

Gloria replied, "No, just up to my waist."

The Bet

A blonde and a redhead met for dinner after work and were watching the 6 o'clock news. A man was shown threatening to jump from the Brooklyn Bridge. The blonde bet the redhead $50 that he wouldn't jump, and the redhead replied, "I'll take that bet!"

Anyway, sure enough, he jumped, so the blonde gave the redhead the $50 she owned. The redhead said, "I can't take this, you're my friend." The blonde said, "No. A bet's a bet."

So the redhead said, "Listen, I have to admit, I saw this one on the 5 o'clock news, so I can't take your money." The blonde replied, "Well, so did I, but I never thought he'd jump again!"

Let's Take A Trip To Disney

Two blondes had driven across the country to see Disney World in Florida.

As they approached it and got onto the final stretch of highway, they saw a sign saying "Disney World Left!"

After thinking for a minute, the driver blonde said "Oh well!" and started driving back home.

Ventriloquist

A young ventriloquist is touring the clubs and one night he's doing a show in a small town in Arkansas.

With his dummy on his knee, he starts going through his usual dumb blonde jokes when a blonde in the 4th row stands on her chair and starts shouting: "I've heard enough of your stupid blonde jokes. What makes you think you can stereotype women that way? What does the color of a person's hair have to do with her worth as a human being? It's guys like you who keep women like me from being respected at work and in the community and from reaching our full potential as a person. Because you and your kind continue to perpetuate discrimination against not only blondes, but women in general, and all in the name of humor!"

The embarrassed ventriloquist begins to apologize, and the blonde yells, "You stay out of this, mister! I'm talking to that little shit on your knee."

Buying Drinks at a Bar

A blonde, a brunette and a redhead went into a bar and ordered their drinks from the bartender.

Brunette: "I'll have a B and C."

Bartender:"What is a B and C?".

Brunette: "Bourbon and Coke."

Redhead: "And, I'll have a G and T."

Bartender: "What's a G and T?"

Redhead: "Gin and tonic."

Blonde: "I'll have a 15."

Bartender: "What's a 15?"

Blonde: "7 and 7"

Pedestrians and Catholics

The traffic light wasn't working on the corner of Broadway and 72nd Street, so the blonde stood with a large crowd of people waiting to cross, while a cop directed traffic.

Finally, the cop blew his whistle, motioned to the crowd, and shouted, "Okay, pedestrians!" The throng surged across Broadway -- all except the blonde, who stayed on the corner.

When the walkers were safely on the other side of the street, the cop moved the cross-traffic through the intersection. Half a minute later, he stopped the cars on Broadway and sent the 72nd Street traffic into motion.

Again, he got around to the blonde's corner, where by this time she had again been joined by a crowd of people.

Tweeeeeeeet! "Okay, pedestrians!"

The crowd crossed the street, but again the blonde stayed put. She looked at her watch and tapped her foot but never budged from the sidewalk.

Finally, after the cop yelled "Okay, pedestrians!" for the third time, the blonde shouted across traffic, "Yo! Officer! Isn't it about time you let the Catholics cross?"

One Wish To Each

Three blondes were walking through the desert when they found a magic genie's lamp.

After rubbing the lamp to make the genie appear, he said, "I will grant three wishes, one for each of you."

The first said, "I wish I were smarter."

So, she became a redhead.

The second blonde said, "I wish I were smarter than she is."

She became a brunette.

The third blond ordered, "I wish I were smarter than both of them!"

So, she became a man.

The Blonde Farmer

A man is driving down a country road, when he spots a farmer standing in the middle of a huge field of grass. Of course the farmer is a blonde.

He pulls the car over to the side of the road and notices that the farmer is just standing there, doing nothing, looking at nothing.

The man gets out of the car, walks all the way out to the farmer and asks him, "Ah excuse me mister, but what are you doing?"

The farmer replies, "I'm trying to win a Nobel Prize."

"How?" asks the man, puzzled.

"Well, I heard they give the Nobel Prize to people who are out standing in their field!"

Losing Your Load

As a trucker stops for a red light, a blonde catches up. She jumps out of her car, runs up to his truck, and knocks on the door. The trucker lowers the window, and she says "Hi, my name is Heather and you are losing some of your load."

The trucker ignores her and proceeds down the street. When the truck stops for another red light, the girl catches up again. She jumps out of her car, runs up and knocks on the door.

Again, the trucker lowers the window. As if they've never spoken, the blonde says brightly,
"Hi my name is Heather, and you are losing some of your load!" Shaking his head, the trucker ignores her again and continues down the street.

At the third red light, the same thing happens again. All out of breath, the blonde gets out of her car, runs up, knocks on the truck door. The trucker rolls down the window. Again she says
"Hi, my name is Heather, and you are losing some of your load!"

When the light turns green the trucker revs up and races to the next light. When he stops this time, he hurriedly gets out of the truck, and runs back to the blonde. He knocks on her window, and after she lowers it, he says... "Hi, my name is Kevin, it's winter in Pennsylvania and I'm driving the SALT TRUCK!"

Yell for Help

Three blondes are in an elevator when the elevator suddenly stops and the lights go out. They try using their cell phones to get help, but have no luck. Even the phones are out.

After a few hours of being stuck with no help in sight, one blonde says to the others "I think the best way to call for help is by yelling together."

The others agree with the first, so they all inhale deeply and begin to yell loudly "Together, together, together."

Only Three Doors

An airline captain was breaking in a new blonde stewardess. The route they were flying had a layover in another city. Upon their arrival, the captain showed the stewardess the best place for airline personnel to eat, shop and stay overnight.

The next morning, as the pilot was preparing the crew for the day's route, he noticed the new stewardess was missing. He knew which room she was in at the hotel and called her up wondering what happened. She answered the phone, crying, and said she couldn't get out of her room. "You can't get out of your room?" the captain asked, "Why not?"

The stewardess replied: "There are only three doors in here," she sobbed, "one is the bathroom, one is the closet, and one has a sign on it that says 'Do Not Disturb'!"

Make It Off the Island

There were three people stranded on an island, a brunette, a redhead, and a blonde. The brunette looked over the water to the mainland and estimated about 20 miles to shore. So she announced, "I'm going to try to swim to shore." So she swam out five miles, and got really tired. She swam out ten miles from the island, and she was too tired to go on, so she drowned.

The second one, the redhead, said to herself, "I wonder if she made it. I guess it's better to try to get to the mainland than stay here and starve." So she attempts to swim out. The redhead had a lot more endurance than the brunette, as she swam out 10 miles before she even got tired. After 15 miles, she was too tired to go on, so she drowned.

So the blonde thought to herself, "I wonder if they made it! I think I'd better try to make it, too." So she swam out 5 miles, ten miles, fifteen miles, and finally nineteen miles from the island. The shore was just in sight, but she said, "I'm too tired to go on!" So she swam back.

Your Kid Has Been Kidnapped

A blonde, out of money and down on her luck after buying air at a real bargain, needed money desperately. To raise cash, she decided to kidnap a child and hold him for ransom.

She went to the local playground, grabbed a kid randomly, took her behind a building, and told her, "I've kidnapped you."

She then wrote a big note saying, "I've kidnapped your kid. Tomorrow morning, put $10,000 in a paper bag and leave it under the apple tree next to the slides on the south side of the playground. Signed, A blonde."

The blonde then pinned the note to the kid's shirt and sent him home to show it to his parents. The next morning the blonde checked, and sure enough, a paper bag was sitting beneath the apple tree. The blonde looked in the bag and found the $10,000 with a note that said, "How could you do this to a fellow blonde?"

Horrific Accident

A blonde had just totaled her car in a horrific accident. Miraculously, she managed to pry herself from the wreckage without a scratch and was applying fresh lipstick when the state trooper arrived.

"My God!" the trooper gasped. "Your car looks like an accordion that was stomped on by an elephant. Are you OK ma'am?"

"Yes, officer, I'm just fine" the blonde chirped.

"Well, how in the world did this happen?" the officer asked as he surveyed the wrecked car.

"Officer, it was the strangest thing!" the blonde began. I was driving along this road when from out of nowhere this TREE pops up in front of me. So I swerved to the right, and there was another tree! I swerved to the left and there was ANOTHER tree! I served to the right and there was another tree! I swerved to the left and there was ...."

"Uh, ma'am", the officer said, cutting her off, "There isn't a tree on this road for 30 miles. That was your air freshener swinging back and forth."

Slot Machine Winner

A dumb blonde was standing in front of a soda machine outside of a local store. After putting in one dollar, a root beer pops out of the machine. She set it on the ground, puts one more dollar into the machine, and pushes another button; suddenly, a coke comes out the machine!

She continued to do this until a man waiting to use the machine became impatient. "Excuse me, can I get my soda and then you can go back to whatever stupid thing you are doing?"

The blonde turns around and says, "Yeah right! I'm not giving up this machine while I'm still winning!"

Look at the Dog

Two blondes are walking down the road, when one says, "Look at that dog with one eye!"

The other blonde covers one of her eyes and says, "Where?"

The Video Rental

A blonde named Mary decides to do something really wild. Something she hasn't done before, so she goes out to rent her first X-rated adult video.

She goes to the video store, and after looking around for a while, selects a title that sounds very stimulating.

She drives home, lights some candles, slips into something comfortable, and puts the tape in the VCR.

To her disappointment, there's nothing but static on the screen, so she calls the video store to complain.

"I just rented an adult movie from you and there's nothing on the tape but static," she says.

"Sorry about that. We've had problems with some of those tapes. Which title did you rent?" the clerk replies.

"Head Cleaner," Mary replies.

Blind Man

A blind man enters a lady's bar by mistake. Finding his way to the bar, he orders a drink. After a few drinks he yells, "Does anybody want to hear a blonde joke?"

The place gets silent. Then a woman with a deep, husky voice sitting to the right of the man says, "Sir, since you are blind, I think it is only fair to let you know that

The bartender is a blonde woman.

The bouncer is a blonde woman.

The woman on your left is blonde and a professional wrestler.

I'm a six foot tall blonde woman with a black belt in karate.

The woman next to me is blonde and a professional weight lifter.

Do you still want to tell that joke?"

"Nah," says the man. "Not if I'm gonna have to explain it FIVE times."

She Was Soooo Blonde...

- She thought a quarterback was a refund.
- She thought General Motors was in the army.
- She thought Meow Mix was a CD for cats.
- She thought Boyz II Men was a day care center.
- At the bottom of an application where it says 'Sign here:' she wrote 'Sagittarius.'
- She took the ruler to bed to see how long she slept.
- She sent a fax with a stamp on it.
- Under 'education' on her job application, she put 'Hooked On Phonics.'
- She tripped over a cordless phone.
- She spent 20 minutes looking at the orange juice can because it said 'Concentrate.'
- She told me to meet her at the corner of 'WALK' and 'DON'T WALK.'
- She tried to put M&M's in alphabetical order.
- She studied for a blood test.
- She sold the car for gas money.
- When she missed bus #44 she took bus #22 twice instead.
- When she went to the airport and saw a sign that said, 'Airport Left,' she turned around and went home.
- When she heard that 90% of all crimes occur around the home, she moved.
- She thought if she spoke her mind, she'd be speechless.
- She thought that she could not use her AM radio in

the evening.

- She had a shirt that said 'TGIF,' which she thought stood for 'This Goes In Front.'

- She thought Taco Bell was the Mexican phone company.

Parachute Jumping

On the first day of training for parachute jumping, a blonde listened intently to the instructor. He told them to start preparing for landing when they are at 300 feet.

The blonde asked, "How am I supposed to know when I'm at 300 feet?"

"That's a good question. When you get to 300 feet, you can recognize the faces of people on the ground."

After pondering his answer, she asked, "What happens if there's no one there I know?"

How Many Sheep Do I Have?

There once was a blonde who was very tired of blonde jokes and insults directed at her intelligence.

So, she cut and dyed her hair, got a make-over, got in her car, and began driving around in the country.

Suddenly, she came to a herd of sheep in the road. She stopped her car and went over to the shepherd who was tending to them.

"If I can guess the exact number of sheep here, will you let me have one?" she asked.

The shepherd, thinking this was a pretty safe bet, agreed.

"You have 171 sheep," said the blonde in triumph.

Surprised, the shepherd told her to pick out a sheep of her choice.

She looked around for a while and finally found one that she really liked.

She picked it up and was petting it when the shepherd walked over to her and asked, "If I can guess your real hair color, will you give me my sheep back?"

The blonde thought it was only fair to let him try. "You're a blonde! Now give me back my dog."

Diamond Ring

A cop saw a young blonde woman down on her knees under a streetlight. "Can I help you?" he asked.

Replied the woman, "I dropped my diamond ring and I'm looking for it."

Asked the cop "Did you drop it right here?"

"No," responded the blonde, "I dropped it about a block away, but the light's better here."

Acute Appendicitis

A blonde was having sharp pains in her side. The doctor examined her and said, "You have acute appendicitis."

The blond yelled at the doctor... "I came here to get medical help, not get a stupid compliment!"

Helping An Overweight Blonde

An overweight blonde consulted her doctor for advice. The doctor advised that she run ten miles a day for thirty days. This, he promised, would help her lose as many as twenty pounds.

The blonde followed the doctor's advice, and, after thirty days, she was pleased to find that she had indeed lost the pesky twenty pounds. She phoned the doctor and thanked him for the wonderful advice which produced such effective results.

At the end of the conversation, however, she asked one last question: "How do I get home, since I am now 300 miles away?"

Guess Who Knows the State Capitals?

A dumb blonde was bragging about her knowledge of the state capitals of the United States. She proudly announced, "go ahead, ask me any of the capitals, I know all of them."

A redhead said, "O.K., what's the capital of Wyoming?"

The blonde replied, "Oh, that's easy, 'W'."

Ironing Phone Call

A blonde with two red ears went to her doctor.

The doctor asked her "What happened?"

She answered, "I was ironing a shirt and the phone rang, but instead of picking up the phone I accidentally picked up the iron and stuck it to my ear."

"Oh Dear!" the doctor exclaimed in disbelief. "But what happened to your other ear?"

"The person called back."

Jealous Revenge

A blonde suspects her boyfriend of cheating on her, so she goes out and buys a gun. She goes to his apartment unexpectedly and sure enough, she opens the door and finds him in the arms of a redhead.

Well, the blonde is angry, she opens her purse to take out the gun but as she does so, she is overcome with grief. She takes the gun and puts it to her head.

The boyfriend yells "No, honey, don't do it."

The blonde replies "Shut up, you're next."

I'm Going Ice Fishing!

A blonde who got a fishing rod for her birthday decided to go ice fishing to make good use of her gift. Early the next morning, she got all her gear together and headed out to the ice.

When she reached her final destination, she cut a large hole in the ice and dipped the rod in. Then suddenly she heard a voice that said: "There are no fish in there".

So she moves to another spot and cuts another hole, but then the same voice spoke again and told her there were no fish in there.

So she moves again, and the voice tells her there are no fish in there. So she looks up and sees an irritated man staring down at her.

"How do you know there are no fish there?" asks the blonde.

So the man cooly says "Well first of all, this is a hockey rink, and second of all, you're going to have to pay for those holes."

The Blonde and the Lottery

A blonde woman finds herself in dire trouble. Her business has gone bust and she's in serious financial trouble. She's so desperate that she decides to ask God for help.

She begins to pray... "God, please help me. I've lost my business and if I don't get some money, I'm going to lose my house as well. Please let me win the lotto."

Lotto night comes and somebody else wins it.

She again prays "God, please let me win the lotto! I've lost my business, my house and I'm going to lose my car as well."

Lotto night comes and she still has no luck.

Once again, she prays... "My God, why have you forsaken me? I've lost my business, my house, and my car. My children are starving. I don't often ask you for help and I have always been a good servant to you. PLEASE just let me win the lotto this one time so I can get my life back in order."

Suddenly there is a blinding flash of light as the heavens open and she is confronted by the voice of God Himself: "At least meet me halfway on this -- buy a ticket."

Blonde Police Applicants

Three blondes were all applying for the last available position on the Texas Highway Patrol.

The detective conducting the interview looked at the three of them and said, "So y'all want to be cops, huh?"

The blondes all nodded.

The detective got up, opened a file drawer and pulled out a folder. Sitting back down, he opened it and pulled out a picture, and said,

"To be a detective, you have to be able to detect. You must be able to notice things such as distinguishing features and oddities, such as scars and so forth."

So saying, he stuck the photo in the face of the first blonde and withdrew it after about two seconds. "Now," he said, "did you notice any distinguishing features about this man?"

The blonde immediately said, "Yes, I did. He has only one eye!"

The detective shook his head and said, "Of course he has only one eye in this picture! It's a profile of his face! You're dismissed!"

The first blonde hung her head and walked out of the office.

The detective then turned to the second blonde, stuck the photo in her face for two seconds, pulled it back and said, "What about you? Notice anything unusual or outstanding about this man?"

"Yes! He only has one ear!"

The detective put his head in his hands and exclaimed,

"Didn't you hear what I just told the other lady? This is a profile of the man's face! Of course you can only see one ear!! You're excused too!"

The second blonde sheepishly walked out of the office.

The detective turned his attention to the third and last blonde and said, "This is probably a waste of time, but..." He flashed the photo in her face for a couple of seconds and withdrew it, saying, "All right, did you notice anything distinguishing or unusual about this man?"

The blonde said, "I sure did. This man wears contact lenses."

The detective frowned, took another look at the picture and began looking at some of the papers in the folder.

He looked up at the blonde with a puzzled expression and said, "You're absolutely right! His bio says he wears contacts! How in the world could you tell that by looking at his picture? "

The blonde rolled her eyes and said, "Well, Helloooo! With only one ear, he certainly can't wear glasses."

Car Problems

A blonde pushes her BMW into a gas station. She tells the mechanic it died. After he works on it for a few minutes, it is idling smoothly.

She says, "What's the story?"

He replies, "Just crap in the carburetor."

She asks, "How often do I have to do that?"

A Blonde Astronaut

There was a blonde, a redhead, and a brunette and they were all up in space.

Each girl tried thinking up ways to be better then the other two...

The redhead said, "I am going to be the first woman to land on mars."

The brunette said, "I can beat that, I'll be the first woman to land on saturn."

The blonde said, "I'll beat both of you, I'll be the first woman to land on the sun."

"How are you going to do that", the other two asked.

"Simple", said the blonde. "I'll go at night!"

Bowling Team

Two bowling teams, one of all blondes and one of all brunettes, charter a double-decker bus for a weekend bowling tournament in Atlantic City. The Brunette team rides in the bottom of the bus. The Blonde team rides on the top level.

The Brunette team down below is whooping it up having a great time, when one of them realises she doesn't hear anything from the blondes upstairs.

She decides to go up and investigate. When the brunette reaches the top, she finds all the blondes frozen in fear, staring straight-ahead at the road, and clutching the seats in front of them with white knuckles.

She says, "What the heck's goin' on up here? We're havin' a grand time downstairs!" One of the blondes looks up and says, "Yeah, but you've got a driver!"

The Blonde Test Taker

A blonde reports for her university final exam which consists of mainly true and false questions. She takes her seat in the examination hall, stares at the question paper for five minutes, and then in a fit of inspiration takes her purse out, removes a coin and starts tossing the coin and marking the answer sheet: true for heads and false for tails. Within thirty minutes she is all done, whereas the rest of the class is still working furiously.

During the last few minutes, she is seen desperately throwing the coin, swearing and sweating. The moderator, alarmed, approaches her and asks what is happening.

"I finished the exam in a half hour," she replies. "Now I'm rechecking my answers."

Dumb Blonde Crooks

Two blonde robbers were robbing a hotel. The first one said, "I hear sirens. Jump!"

The second one said, "But we're on the 13th floor!"

The first one screamed back, "This is no time to be superstitious."

Blondes Change A Light Bulb

Three blondes are attempting to change a light bulb. One of them decides to call 911:

Blonde: We need help. We're three blondes changing a light bulb.

Operator: Hmmmmm. You put in a fresh bulb?

Blonde: Yes.

Operator: The power in the house in on?

Blonde: Of course.

Operator: And the switch is on?

Blonde: Yes, yes.

Operator: And the bulb still won't light up?

Blonde: No, it's working fine.

Operator: Then what's the problem?

Blonde: We got dizzy spinning the ladder around, and we all fell and hurt ourselves.

Swim the English Channel

There was a blonde, a brunette, and a redhead standing on the beach. They had decided the previous evening whilst in the pub to try and swim the English channel. After some discussion, they decided the quickest way would be to do the breast stroke, so off they set.

One day later the redhead reached the French coast. Having lost sight of the other two swimmers just off the English coast she decided that they couldn't be far behind so sat on the beach looking out to sea waiting for the other two.

After a cold night of waiting, the brunette finally came into sight. "What took you so long?" inquired the redhead.

"There were some strong currents out there! But I'm here now! Am I the last?" replied the brunette.

"No. Blondie is still out there somewhere." They decided to wait.

Day after day the two swimmers sat on the beach until on the 5th day Blondie came into view. Once on dry land the brunette asked the blonde "What took you so long?"

"What do you expect? You guy's cheated, replied the indignant blonde, "You used your hands!"

Blonde Locked Out

This blonde walked into a party store and asked the cashier if he had a hanger or something to unlock her car because she locked her keys in the car. He nodded and handed her a hanger. She thanked him and went outside to set to work.

A little while later the cashier decided to check on her and saw her working at it and another blonde in the car was saying "a little to the left... no, a little to the right..."

Applying For A Job

A blonde was filling out a job application form. She quickly filled out the columns entitled: Name, Age, Address, etc.

Finally, she came to the column: Salary Expected.

She wrote, "YES."

Blonde Cops

A blonde cop stops blonde motorist and asks for her driving license.

The motorist scuffles around in her purse and can't find it. She says to the cop, "I must have left it at home officer."

The cop says, "Well, do you have any kind of identification?" The motorist scuffles around in her purse again, and finds a pocket mirror.

She looks at it and says to the cop, "All I have is this picture of myself." The cop says, "Let me see it, then." So the blonde motorist gives the mirror to the blonde cop, who looks at it, and replies, "Well, if I had known you were a police officer, I wouldn't have even pulled you over. You can go now."

Polish Priest

A blonde was telling a priest a Polish joke, when halfway through the priest interrupts her, "Don't you know I'm Polish?"

"Oh, I'm sorry," the blonde apologizes, "Do you want me to start over and talk slower?"

You've Got Mail

A man was in his front yard mowing grass when his attractive blonde neighbor came out of the house and went straight to the mailbox. She opened it then slammed it shut and stormed back into the house. A little later she came out of her house again, went to the mailbox and again opened it, and slammed it shut again. Angrily, back into the house she went.

As the man was getting ready to edge the lawn, she came out again, marched to the mailbox, opened it and then slammed it closed harder than ever.

Puzzled by her actions the man asked her, "Is something wrong?"

To which she replied, "There certainly is!"

My stupid computer keeps saying, "You've got mail!"

Sell That Car Easier

A blonde made several attempts to sell her old car. She was having a lot of problems finding a buyer because the car had 340,000 miles on it. She discussed her problem with a brunette that she worked with at a bar.

The brunette suggested, "There may be a chance to sell that car easier, but it's not going to be legal."

"That doesn't matter at all," replied the blonde. "All that matters it that I am able to sell this car."

"Alright," replied the brunette. In a quiet voice, she told the blonde: "Here is the address of a friend of mine. He owns a car repair shop around here. Tell him I sent you, and he will turn the counter back on your car to 40,000 miles. Then it shouldn't be a problem to sell your car."

The following weekend, the blonde took a trip to the mechanic on the brunette's advice.

About one month after that, the brunette saw the blonde and asked, "Did you sell your car?"

"No!" replied the blonde. "Why should I? It only has 40,000 miles on it."

Do You Know Where You Were Going?

A policeman pulled a blonde over after she'd been driving the wrong way on a one-way street.

Cop: Do you know where you were going?

Blonde: No, but wherever it is, it must be bad because all the cars were leaving.

Cutting Pizza

A blonde went to buy a Pizza and after ordering, the assistant asked the blonde if she would like her pizza cut into six pieces or twelve.

"Six please" she said, "I could never eat twelve!"

Short Questions and Answers

Q: What did the blonde think of the new computer?
A: She didn't like it because she couldn't get MTV.

Q: What's a dumb blonde favorite rock group?
A: Air Supply.

Q: Why do blondes put their hair in ponytails?
A: To cover up the valve stem.

Q: How many blondes does it take to change a light bulb?
A: Two. 1 to hold the Diet Irn-Bru and the other to call on 'Daddddyyy'.

Q: Why did the blonde keep a coat hanger in her back seat?
A: In case she locks the keys in her car.

Q: What do you call the blonde in a horror movie?
A: Dead meat.

Q. Why don't blondes eat pickles?
A. Because they can't get their head in the jar.

Q. What do you call a basement full of blondes?
A. A wine cellar.

Q: What's the definition of eternity?
A: 4 blondes at a 4 way stop.

Q. What's the blonde's cheer?
A. " I'm blonde, I'm blonde, I'm B.L.O.N....ah, oh well.. I'm blonde, I'm blonde, yea yea yea..."

Q. Why did the blonde drive into the ditch?
A. To turn the blinker off.

Q: How do you measure their intelligence?
A: Stick a tire pressure gauge in their ear.

Q: What does a blonde Owl say?
A: What, what?

Q: How do you tell if a blonde writes Mysteries?
A: She's got a checkbook.

Q: How do you hit a blonde and she will never know it?
A: With a thought.

Q: Why did the blonde keep failing her driver's test?
A: Because every time the door opened, she jumped into the back seat.

Q: What do you call 10 blondes at the bottom of the pool?
A: Air pockets.

Q: How do you describe a blonde, surrounded by drooling idiots?
A: Flattered.

Q: Why blondes don't have elevator jobs?
A: They don't know the route.

Q: Why did the blonde try and steal a police car?
A: On the back she saw "911" and thought it was a Porsche.

Q: What do you call a blonde on a University Campus?
A: A visitor.

Q: Why do blondes wear earmuffs?
A: To avoid the draft.

Q: How do you drive a blonde insane?
A: Hide her Hair Dryer.

Q: Why do blondes wear shoulder pads?
A: To keep from bruising their ears.

Q: Why can't blondes make ice cubes?
A: Because they don't have the recipe!

Q: What do you call three blondes in a Volkswagen?
A: FARFROMTHINKEN

Q: How many blondes does it take to screw in a light bulb?
A: Two, one to hold the light bulb and one to spin the ladder around!

Q: How does a blonde commit suicide?
A: She gathers her clothes into a pile and jumps off.

Q: How do you confuse a blonde?
A: You don't. They're born that way.

Q: How can you tell which tricycle belongs to the blonde?
A: It is the one with the kickstand.

Q: Why did God create blondes?
A: Cos sheep can't bring beer from the fridge.

Q: How do you make a blonde laugh on Friday?
A: Tell her a joke on Monday!

Q: What do a bowling ball and a blonde have in common?
A: Sooner or later they'll both end up in the gutter.

Q. Why do blondes have little holes all over their faces?
A. From eating with forks.

Q: Have you heard what my blond neighbor wrote on the bottom of her swimming pool?
A: No smoking.

Q: Why are dumb blonde jokes so short?
A: So brunettes can remember them.

Q: How can you tell who a blonde's boyfriend is?
A: He's the one with the belt buckle that matches the impression in her forehead.

Q: How does a blonde spell 'farm'?
A: E-I-E-I-O.

Q: Why did the blonde keep ice cubes in the freezer?
A: So she could keep the refrigerator cold.

Q: How can you tell when a blonde is dating?
A: By the buckle print on her forehead.

Q. What's black and fuzzy and hangs from the ceiling?
A. A blonde electrician.

Q. How do you get a blonde to climb on the roof?
A. Tell her that the drinks are on the house.

Q. What do you call it when a blonde gets taken over by a demon?
A. A vacant possession.

Q. What did the blonde's dentist find?
A. Teeth in the cavity.

Q. What is a blonde doing when she holds her hands tightly over her ears?
A. She's trying to hold on to a thought.

Q. What is a blonde's idea of safe sex?
A. A padded dash.

Q. Why do blondes use white-out on their computer screens?
A. They couldn't find their eraser.

Q. What do you do when a blonde throws a pin at you?
A. Run like hell... she's got a hand grenade in her mouth.

Q. Why did the blonde cross the road?
A. She wanted to see the geese because she heard honking!

Q. Why was the blonde confused after giving birth to twins?
A. She couldn't figure out who the other mother was.

Q. Why did the blonde stare at the frozen orange juice can for hours?
A. Because it said 'concentrate'.

Q. What do blonde virgins eat?
A. Baby food.

Q. Why did the blonde take two hits of acid?
A. She wanted to go on a round trip.

Q. Why did the blonde snort Nutra-Sweet?
A. She thought it was diet coke.

Q: Why was the blonde disappointed with her trip to England?
A: She found out Big Ben is only a clock.

Q: Why do blondes take the pill?
A: So they know what day of the week it is.

Q: What does a postcard from a blonde's vacation say?
A: Having a fantastic time. Where am I?

Q. How does a blonde high-5?
A. She smacks herself in the forehead.

Q: What does "Bones" McCoy say before he performs brain surgery on a blonde?
A: "Space. The final frontier..."

Q. Why did the dumb blonde tattoo her zip code on her stomach?
A. So her male would get delivered to the right box.

Q: Why do blondes have TGIF written on their shoes?
A: Toes Go In First.

Q: What do SMART blondes and UFOs have in common?
A: You always hear about them but never see them.

Q: Why do blondes always smile during lightning storms?
A: They think their picture is being taken.

Q: How can you tell if a blonde is a good cook?
A: Manages to get the Pop Tarts out the toaster in one piece.

Q: What does a blonde do first thing in the morning?
A: She goes home!

Q: What happens when a blonde gets Alzheimer's disease?
A: Her IQ goes up!

Q: What does a blonde do when someone says its chili outside?
A: She grabs a bowl.

Q: Why do blondes wear green lipstick?
A: Because red means stop.

Q: What does a blond and a beer bottle have in common?
A: They're both empty from the neck up.

Q: What goes VROOM, SCREECH, VROOM, SCREECH, VROOM, SCREECH?
A: A blonde going through a flashing red light.

Q: Why can't you tell blondes knock-knock jokes?
A: Because they go answer the door.

Q: Why don't blondes like making KOOL-AID?
A: Because they can't fit 8 cups of water in the little packet.

Q: Why are blondes hurt by people's words?
A: Because people keep hitting them with dictionaries.

Q: How do you get a blonde eyes to twinkle?
A: Shine a flash light in her ears.

Q: Did you hear about the blonde who stood in front of a mirror with her eyes closed?
A: She wanted to see what she looked like asleep.

Q: What do you see when you look directly into a blonde's eyes?
A: The back of her head.

Q: Why don't blondes double recipes?
A: The oven doesn't go to 700 degrees.

Q: What did the blonde do when she missed the 66 bus?
A: She took the 33 bus twice instead.

Q: What do you call a blonde behind a steering wheel?
A: An air bag.

Q: Why does a blonde only change her baby's diapers every month?
A: Because it says on the box: "good for up to 20 pounds."

Q: What's the difference between blondes and McDonald's?
A: A blonde serves more people in a night.

Q: What is the difference between a blonde and "The Titanic"?
A: They know how many men went down on "The Titanic".

Q: Did you hear about the dumb blonde couple that were found frozen to death in their car at a drive-in movie theater?
A: They went to see "Closed for the Winter".

Q: Why did the blonde have tire tread marks on her back?
A: From crawling across the street when the sign said "DON'T WALK".

Q: Why did the blonde tip-toe past the medicine cabinet?
A: So she wouldn't wake up the sleeping pills.

Q: Why did the blonde wear condoms on her ears?
A: So she wouldn't get Hearing Aides.

Q: Why did the blonde scale the glass wall?
A: To see what was on the other side.

Q: Why did the blonde want to become a veterinarian?
A: Because she loved children.

Q: Why did the blonde take her typewriter to the doctor?
A: She thought it was pregnant because missed a period.

Q. Why did the blonde nurse take a red magic marker to work?
A. In case she had to draw some blood.

Q: Did you hear about the blonde coyote?
A: Got stuck in a trap, chewed off three legs and was still stuck.

Q: What do you call it when a blonde dies their hair brunette?
A: Artificial intelligence.

Q: Why is it good to have a blonde passenger?
A: You can park in the handicap zone.

Q: A one armed blonde is hanging from a tree. How can you make her fall?
A: You wave at her!

Q: What's the difference between a smart blonde and Bigfoot?
A: Maybe someday we'll find Bigfoot.

Q: What would you do if a blonde threw a hand grenade right at you?
A: You'd pull the pin and throw it back.

Q: How do you get a blonde to stay in the shower all day?
A: Lend her your bottle of Shampoo that says "lather, rinse, repeat".

Q: What do you call 10 blondes standing ear to ear?
A: A wind tunnel.

Q. How does a blonde kill a fish?
A. She drowns it.

Q: What do you call a really smart blonde?
A: A golden retriever.

Q: What did the blonde say when she saw the sign in front of the YMCA?
A: "Look! They spelled MACY'S wrong!"

Q: Did you hear the one about the blonde who had a bumper sticker that said, "ALL BLONDES AREN'T DUMB?"
A: No one could read it because it was hung upside-down.

Q: Why did the blonde have square boobs?
A: Because she forgot to take the tissues out of the box.

Q: What did the blonde say when she looked into a box of Cheerios?
A: "Oh look! Donut seeds!"

Q: Why does it take longer to build a blonde snowman than a regular one?
A: You have to hollow out the head.

Q: Why do blondes work seven days a week?
A: So you don't have to retrain them on Monday.

Q: How do you plant dope?
A: Bury a blonde.

Q: How do you make a blonde's eyes light up?
A: Shine a flashlight in their ear.

Q: How do you kill a blonde?
A: Put spikes in their shoulder pads.

Q: How do you drown a blonde?
A: Put a mirror at the bottom of the pool.

Q: Why do blondes hate M&Ms?
A: They're too hard to peel.

Q: How do you drive a blonde crazy?
A: Give her a bag of M&Ms and tell her to alphabetize them.

Q: How do you know when a blonde has been making chocolate chip cookies?
A: You find M&M shells all over the kitchen floor.

Q: What job function does a blonde have in an M&M factory?
A: Proofreading.

Q: Why couldn't the blonde write the number eleven?
A: She didn't know what number came first.

Q: What do you call a blonde with 90% of her intelligence gone?
A: Divorced.

Q: How did the blonde try to kill the bird?
A: She threw it off a cliff.

Q: How did the blonde break her leg raking leaves?
A: She fell out of the tree.

Q: How did the blonde die drinking milk?
A: The cow fell on her.

Q: How did the blonde burn her nose?
A: Bobbing for french fries.

Q: Why did it take the blonde seven days to drive from St. Louis to Chicago?
A: She kept seeing signs that read "stop clean bathroom".

Q: How can you tell if a blonde's been using the computer?
A: There's white-out on the screen.

Q: How can you tell if another blonde's been using the computer?
A: There's writing on the white-out.

Q: How can you tell when a fax had been sent from a blonde?
A: There is a stamp on it.

Q: Why should blondes not be given coffee breaks?
A: It takes too long to retrain them.

Q: Why do blondes drive BMWs?
A: Because they can spell it.

Q: Why do blondes wear their hair up?
A: To catch as much as they can that is over their heads.

Q: Why don't blondes make good pharmacists?
A: They can't get the bottle into the typewriter.

Q: Why don't blondes call 911 in an emergency?
A: They can't remember the number.

Q: Why don't blondes call 911 in an emergency?
A: She can't find the number 11 on the telephone buttons.

Q: How many blondes does it take to change a light bulb?
A: "What's a light bulb?"

Q: How do you get rid of blondes?
A: Form a circle, give each blonde a gun, and tell them they are a firing squad.

Q: Santa Claus, the Tooth Fairy, a dumb blonde, and a smart blonde are walking down the street when they spot a $10 bill. Who picks it up?
A: The dumb blonde! because, there is no such thing as Santa Claus, the Tooth Fairy, or a smart blonde.

Q: Santa Claus, the Tooth Fairy, a dumb blonde, and a smart blonde are walking down the street when they spot a $10 bill. Who picks it up?
A: None of them, two don't exist and the dumb blonde thought it was a gum wrapper.

Q: If a blonde and a brunette are tossed off a building, who hits the ground first?
A: The brunette. The blonde has to stop to ask for directions.

Q: What does a blonde make best for dinner?
A: Reservations.

Q: What do you get when you offer a blonde a penny for her thoughts?
A: Change.

Q: What does a blonde say if you blow in his/her ear?
A: "Thanks for the refill!"

Q: What do you call a dumb blonde behind a steering wheel?
A: An Air Bag.

Q: What do you call a blonde between two brunettes?
A: A mental block.

Q: What do you call 15 blondes in a circle?
A: A dope ring.

Q: What do you call an unmarried blonde in a BMW?
A: Divorcee'

Q: What do you call a blonde with 2 brain cells?
A: Pregnant.

Q: Why did the blonde scale the chain-link fence?
A: To see what was on the other side.

Q: Why did the blonde get so excited after she finished her jigsaw puzzle in only 6 months?
A: Because on the box it said from 2-4 years.

Q: Why did the blonde call the welfare office?
A: She wanted to know how to cook food stamps!

Q: Where do blondes go to meet their relatives?
A: The vegetable garden.

Q: What do you call a blonde with half a brain?
A: Gifted!

Q: What do you call a fly buzzing inside a blonde's head?
A: A Space Invader.

Q: What do you call a blonde in a tree with a brief case?
A: Branch Manager.

Q: Why can't blondes put in light bulbs?
A: They keep breaking them with the hammers.

Q: What is a cool refreshing drink for a blonde?
A: Perri-air.

Q: When is it legal to shoot a blonde in the head?
A: When you have a tire pump to reinflate it!

Q: What is it called when a blonde blows in another blonde's ear?
A: Data transfer.

Q: To a blonde, what is long and hard?
A: Grade four.

Q: What is the definition of gross ignorance?
A: 144 blondes.

Q: What did the blonde say to the physicist?
A: "Why, I just love nuclear fission! What do you use for bait?"

Q: A blonde is walking down the street with a pig under her arm. She passes a person who asks "Where did you get that?"
A: The pig says, "I won her in a raffle!"

Q: What did the blonde do when she heard that 90% of accidents occur around the home?
A: She moved.

Q: What's five miles long and has an IQ of forty?
A: A blonde parade.

Q: What is the blonde's highest ambition in life?
A: They want to be like Vanna White and learn the alphabet.

Q: How do you keep a blonde busy all day?
A: Put her in a round room and tell her to sit in the corner.

Q: How do you keep a blonde in suspense?
A: I'll tell you tomorrow.

Q: Why did the blonde put her finger over the nail when she was hammering?
A: The noise gave her a headache.

Q: How does a blond know if she's on her way home or on her way to work?
A: She opens her lunch box to see if there is anything in it.

Q: How do you sink a submarine full of blondes?
A: Knock on the door.

Q: What stops then goes then stops then goes?
A: A blonde at a blinking red light.

Q: Did you hear about Pepsi's new soda just for blondes?
A: It has "open other end" printed on the bottom.

Q: Why do blondes always rapidly flap their hands towards theirs ears?
A: They're refueling.

Q: Why did the blonde purchase an AM radio?
A: She didn't want one for nights.

Q: What about the blonde who gave birth to twins?
A: Her husband is out looking for the other man.

Q: Did you hear about the dead blonde in the closet?
A: She was last years hide and seek winner.

Q: What is dumber than a brunette building a fire under the water?
A: A blonde trying to put it out.

Q: Why did the blonde buy a brown cow?
A: To get chocolate milk.

Q: What do you call a blonde with a brand new PC?
A: A dumb terminal.

Q: How did the blonde burn her ear?
A: The phone rang while she was ironing.

Q: There are 17 blondes standing outside a disco but why couldn't they get in?
A: The sign said "must be 18 to enter".

Q: Why are there no brunette jokes?
A: Because blondes would have to think them up.

Q: How does a blonde make instant pudding?
A: She places the box in the microwave and looks for the "instant pudding setting" button.

Q: Did you hear about the blonde that went to library and checked out a book called "How to Hug"?
A: When she got back to the dorm and found out it was volume seven of the encyclopedia.

Q: What do you call 24 blondes in a cardboard box?
A: A case of empties.

Q: Why are the Japanese so smart?
A: They don't have any blondes.

Q: How does a blonde have safe sex?
A: She locks the car door.

Q. Why does NASA hire peroxide blondes?
A. They're doing research on black holes.

Q. What's the difference between a blonde and a computer?
A. You only have to punch information into a computer once.

Q: What is a blonde's favorite part of a gas station?
A: The Air Pump!

Q: What do peroxide blondes and black men have in common?
A: They both have black roots.

Q: Why didn't the blonde want a window seat on the plane?
A: She'd just blow dried her hair and she didn't want it blown around too much.

Q. Why was the blonde upset when she got her Driver's License?
A. Because she got an F in sex.

Q. What do you call a blonde with a dollar bill on her head?
A. All you can eat under a buck.

Q. Why did the blonde die in a helicopter crash?
A. She got cold and turned off the fan.

Q. What does a blonde say when she gives birth?
A. Gee, are you sure it's mine?

Q. How does a blonde interpret 6.9?
A. A 69 interrupted by a period.

Q. Did you hear about the blonde lesbian?
A. She kept having affairs with men!